Did

NEW

A M

Compiled by Julia Skinner

With particular reference to the work of Nick Channer

THE FRANCIS FRITH COLLECTION

www.francisfrith.com

First published in the United Kingdom in 2006 by The Francis Frith Collection®

This edition published exclusively for Identity Books in 2011 ISBN 978-1-84589-568-6

British Library Cataloguing in Publication Data

Did You Know? Newbury - A Miscellany
Compiled by Julia Skinner
With particular reference to the work of Nick Channer

The Francis Frith Collection
Unit 6, Oakley Business Park,
Wylye Road, Dinton, Wiltshire SP3 5EU
Tel: +44 (0) 1722 716 376
Email: info@francisfrith.co.uk
www.francisfrith.com

Printed and bound in Malaysia

Front Cover: **NEWBURY, NORTHBROOK STREET 1954** N61041p

The colour-tinting is for illustrative purposes only, and is not intended to be historically accurate

CONTENTS

INTRODUCTION

In the Middle Ages Newbury was an important town, with its wealth founded on the cloth trade. It is famous as being the home of Jack O'Newbury, 'the richest clothier in England', and a friend of kings. Newbury is closely associated with two battles in the Civil War. The first battle took place in 1643, and the second battle in 1644 involved gaining possession of the bridge over the Lambourne at Donnington, a mile or so to the north of the town. The remains of Donnington Castle, once an important stronghold, can still be seen.

Newbury's prosperity reached a peak in the 18th century when both the turnpike road and the Kennet & Avon Canal reached the town. However, by the 18th century the cloth industry had moved to Yorkshire and Lancashire, and only sackcloth and sailcloth production remained of Newbury's once great industry. In the 19th century Newbury failed to become an industrial Victorian 'boom town', which probably helped to preserve some of the town's attractive streets and buildings.

Over 100 years ago, Walter Money said in the introduction to his 'History of Newbury' that 'no-one who is a lover of antiquity can fail to walk through Newbury without noticing its ancient gabled houses, too few, alas, but still a sufficient number are left to show us how quaint the old town must have looked before the advent of the many pretentious modern buildings we now see around us'. Many of those 'modern buildings' have either disappeared or mellowed with time and become an accepted part of the fabric of the town. Money's book was published in 1905 and a copy of it was placed beneath the foundation stone of Newbury's former library that year.

Look around and you will see that there is still a great deal of interest in the bustling modern town of Newbury; take a stroll through its winding streets and back alleys and you will discover a wealth of history and architectural interest. The story of Newbury is full of fascinating characters and events, of which this book can only provide a brief glimpse.

THE BANDSTAND, VICTORIA PARK c1965 N61108x

BERKSHIRE DIALECT WORDS AND PHRASES

'Cheeselog' - a woodlouse.

'Deedy' - careful.

'Dout' - to put out a fire.

'Footer' - to cry.

'Shucketty' - shaky.

'Pikked' - pointed.

'Bottom' - a valley.

'Tarblish' - tolerable.

'Snook' - stolen.

'Wuut' - a mole.

'Veatish' - healthy.

'Vorights' - opposite.

HAUNTED NEWBURY

Ghostly echoes from the Civil War are said to haunt Love Lane in Donnington, where a phantom Royalist cavalry patrol re-enacts a skirmish with a Parliamentarian force from Newbury.

The moaning ghost of Thomas Barrie is said to haunt Newbury's Market Place, where in 1538 he was punished for spreading rumours about Henry VIII. His ears were nailed to the town pillory and were then chopped off; Thomas died of shock, and his ghost has roamed the area ever since.

Rooms on the upper floor of 73 Northbrook Street are said to be haunted by the ghost of a Dr Watson, who lived and held his surgery there in the late Victorian period. His ghost was seen on the stairs, which have now been demolished, and was also seen in the rooms, although only from the knees up, as the floors have been raised since the doctor died there in the late 19th century. The ghostly doctor is said to be dressed in a black cloak and top hat, and carries a cane and a black bag. The mysterious sound of a piano being played has also been reported coming from the upstairs rooms, although no one is there - and neither is a piano.

A building on Black Boys Bridge used to be the Vine Inn. It is said to be haunted by the ghost of a former ostler at the inn, and is described as being of a thick-set old man who wears a white shirt and brown or leather jerkin.

Part of the Newbury Bypass is said to be haunted by ghostly figures which have been seen 'floating' along the road. Local lore says that the bypass was built over the site of the First Battle of Newbury of the Civil War and disturbed the mass graves of both Royalist and Parliamentarian soldiers who were killed; their spirits are now unable to rest.

NEWBURY MISCELLANY

Newbury's first inhabitants were probably a group of riverside dwellers who settled here in Mesolithic times. Excavations in the Bartholomew Street and Cheap Street areas seem to confirm that this district was inhabited by hunter-gatherer people six or seven thousand years ago.

Evidence of a late Iron Age farmstead was found during archaeological excavations ahead of construction work on the new Newbury Hospital in 2001 and 2002. No remains of buildings were found, but ditches marked out rectangular fields approached by an ancient trackway. Two cremation burials were also found, dating from the first century AD; one of the burials was accompanied by a pottery plate and knife and three brooches, and the other, which had been disturbed by ploughing, was associated with a pottery cup that appears to have been made in Italy.

During the Roman period, a posting station was established on the Roman road from Silchester to Cirencester at Speen, which was known as Spinae (or Spinis) at that time. Evidence of an important Roman settlement was discovered at Newtown to the south, and there is strong speculation that a significant Roman community existed in Newbury. Relics have come to light in and around the town, most notably in the area around the Market Place. It appears that there was also a Roman cemetery near the goods shed to the north of the town's railway line.

ST NICOLAS'S CHURCH
c1955 N61032f

NO ENTRY

THE VIEW FROM VICTORIA PARK BRIDGE c1955 N61017

A castle is traditionally believed to have once stood in Newbury, where the Wharf was later built. However, archaeological investigations have not found any trace of a castle at the Wharf, and it is more likely to have been sited in Hampstead Marshall. The castle was probably built by John Marshall during the Anarchy, the period of dispute over the succession between King Stephen and his cousin Matilda of the 12th century, and was captured by King Stephen in 1152-53 after a siege lasting more than two months. The siege of the castle (wherever it was sited) was mentioned in 'The History of William the Marshall', where the story is told of the king holding John Marshall's son William as hostage, and threatening to catapult him over the walls when William refused to surrender the castle. John responded with the words 'I have the anvils and the hammer to forge still better sons'. King Stephen's heart was softer though, and he thought better of the idea.

There were once four annual fairs in Newbury: a fair was held on the Day of Annunciation in March, St John the Baptist's Day in June, St Bartholomew's Day in August, and St Jude's Day in October, which survives as the Michaelmas Fair. In the year 1215 King John granted the profits of St Bartholomew's Fair to the almshouses known as St Bartholomew's Hospital.

Newbury has been 'held' by several queens: Henry VIII granted Newbury to two wives, Anne Boleyn, and then Jane Seymour, Elizabeth I held it before her accession, and James I granted Newbury to his queen, Anne of Denmark.

THE LOCK c1955 N61079

THE CLOCK TOWER FROM OXFORD STREET c1955 N61036

The clock tower seen in photograph N61036, partly enclosed
by a hexagonal shelter, stands on the site of a wayside chapel
which was disused in the 16th century, converted into houses
and eventually demolished in 1791. The present clock has
three faces. There was an earlier clock tower on this site,
known as the 'Jubilee Clock', which was erected in 1889 to
commemorate 50 years of Queen Victoria's reign.

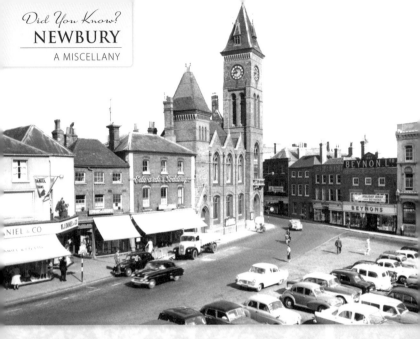

MARKET PLACE c1960 N61084

During the early years of the 15th century, Newbury was held
by Edmund Mortimer, the Earl of March. After his death in 1425,
the town passed to his nephew Richard, Duke of York, bringing
Newbury into the Wars of the Roses, the conflict between rival
claimants to the throne and their supporters. The town was
taken by the Lancastrian Earl of Wiltshire in 1460, when many
of its residents were hanged, drawn and quartered as traitors
for supporting the Yorkists.

The borough of Newbury was granted its first charter by Elizabeth I
on 28 May 1596, and the first mayor was Bartholomew Yate. The 400th
anniversary of this event was marked in 1996 when Her Majesty Queen
Elizabeth II visited the town.

Between the Middle Ages and the 16th century, Berkshire witnessed great activity in the wool and cloth trade, although its decline in the late 16th century caused much unemployment and hardship in the town. Newbury's most famous inhabitant was surely John Winchcombe (sometimes referred to as John Smallwood), better known as Jack O'Newbury, who was described as 'the richest clothier England ever beheld'. Winchcombe was a prosperous medieval businessman who began with nothing, but ended up with over 200 looms, employing over 1,000 men, women and children in a medieval version of a factory system. Winchcombe's cloth 'factory' extended from his home in Northbrook Street to where Victoria Park is now situated.

NORTHBROOK STREET c1954 N61041

There is a story that Jack O'Newbury led 50 horsemen and 50 footmen from Newbury, 'as well armed and better clothed than any', to help the English army fight against the Scots at the Battle of Flodden in 1513, although he may only have recruited and equipped them, rather than actually accompanying them himself. At that time much of the English army was with Henry VIII in France - Queen Katherine sent out an order for all able-bodied men in the country to equip themselves for war, and this number is considerably more than the four men, armed with pikes, and two horsemen for King Henry's service which was Jack's allotted quota. It is not known for sure whether the Newbury men reached the north in time to fight in the battle, in which the Scottish forces were defeated, but an old ballad describes their adventure in glowing detail.

Newbury's historic St Nicolas's Church is one of Berkshire's finest 'wool churches', meaning that it was built from the profits of the wool and cloth industry. The rebuilding of this magnificent Perpendicular church was started by John Winchcombe ('Jack O'Newbury') who died in 1519, and the church was completed in 1532 by his son, also John. There is a fine memorial brass to John Winchcombe the elder (and Alice, his first wife) beneath the tower, which shows him wearing a long fur-lined cloak, with a purse hanging from his belt.

According to legend, Henry VIII offered Jack O'Newbury a knighthood but he turned it down, saying that he preferred to remain the equal of his workers.

DONNINGTON CASTLE
c1955 N61008

Northbrook Street is named after the stream which used to flow along it, but which now flows beneath it in a culvert.

During the Civil War one of the most dramatic periods in Newbury's history occurred. On 20 September 1640, a violent and spectacular battle was fought near the town between the Royalist army and the army of Parliament, led by the Earl of Essex. The bloody encounter, in which 6,000 men died, became known as the First Battle of Newbury. The Second Battle of Newbury took place in 1644 near Donnington Castle, to the north of the town, which at the time of the Civil War belonged to John Packer. His refusal of a loan to Charles I, and his opposition to the king in Parliament, led to the sequestration of his property by the king. Colonel John Boys was sent to take command of the castle for the king in September 1643, with 200 foot, 25 horse and four pieces of cannon. He strengthened the defences of the castle by constructing earthworks around it, which can still be seen today. He withstood two Parliamentarian assaults on the castle in July and September 1644, and was knighted by the king in October 1644, just before the Second Battle of Newbury, which took place later that month. The battle was somewhat inconclusive but the Royalist army was able to slip away, leaving the royal crown, the Great Seal and the artillery in the keeping of Colonel Boys at Donnington. Boys then withstood a siege by the Parliamentarians until he was relieved and provisioned by the king on 9 November. Repeated attempts were made to take the castle, but Boys did not surrender until he was instructed by the king to do so on 1 April 1646. Most of the castle was demolished later in the same year by order of Parliament; the only feature still standing is its splendid four-towered gatehouse, seen in photograph N61008, opposite.

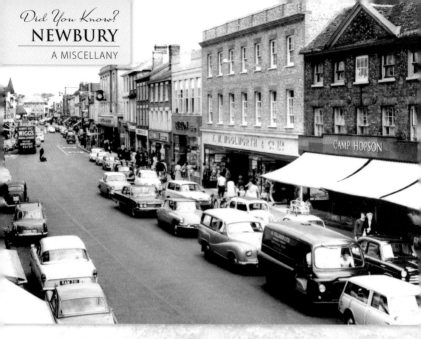

NORTHBROOK STREET c1965 N61111

Marks & Spencer now stands on the site of Jack O'Newbury's former home in Northbrook Street. Jack and his wife regularly entertained some of the most prominent people in Tudor England, most notably Henry VIII and Katherine of Aragon, at which time Jack is said to have covered the floor of his house with blue cloth. Only one gable end of Jack's actual house has survived (in Marsh Lane), but it is an important example of 16th-century brick and timber architecture, including a fine oriel window.

The 17th-century side-saddle traveller Celia Fiennes visited Newbury and said that it was 'a little town famous for makeing the best whipps'.

In 1556, during the reign of the Roman Catholic Queen Mary, three men known as the Newbury Martyrs were burnt at the stake for their Protestant beliefs. The men, Julius Palmer (sometimes referred to as Julins, or Joscelyn), Thomas Askew and John Gwin, were executed for heresy off the Enborne Road, near the Lamb Inn.

St Nicolas's Church was used by Parliamentarian troops as a guardroom and hospital during the Civil War of the 17th century. Much of the church was vandalised and defaced at this time, with lead stripped from the nave and aisle roofs; even the weathercock was pulled down.

ST NICOLAS'S CHURCH c1955 N61037f

The Town Bridge, shown in photograph N16046, below, was built before the Kennet & Avon Canal, so there is no towpath. Access to Northbrook Street and the eastern side of the canal is via a narrow passage running beneath the buildings on the left of the photograph. The present bridge, which is noted for its stone dressings and balustrades, was completed in 1772 at a cost of

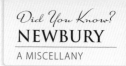
more than £700; it replaced two wooden structures, one of which was destroyed by floods in 1726. Its strength was put to the test during the Second World War when tanks and other heavy vehicles were constantly crossing it. A pub called the Lock, Stock and Barrel now occupies the site by the footbridge.

THE TOWN BRIDGE OVER THE RIVER KENNET c1955 N61046

In the 18th century a chambermaid at the Pelican Inn at Speenhamland called Anne was unhappily married to a Mr Jeffries, an ostler at the inn. One evening Henry Bridges, 2nd Duke of Chandos, was dining at the inn when he heard a commotion outside in the yard and was told that 'A man is going to sell his wife and they are leading her up the yard with a halter round her neck'. On investigation the duke found that Jeffries was offering his wife for sale, and he was so struck by her beauty that he bought her himself. Anne was the duke's mistress for many years, and married him in 1744, the duke's wife and Mr Jeffries having both died by then. However, not everyone was as impressed with Anne, the new Duchess of Chandos. Soon after the marriage, Lord Omery commented: 'Of her person and character people speak variously, but all agree that both are very bad'.

The Pelican Inn at Speenhamland was the setting in 1795 for a meeting of Berkshire magistrates which has gone down in history as the introduction of the Speenhamland System. This was a way of calculating the poor relief that should be paid from the local parish rates by tying the amount of relief payments to the cost of a loaf of bread, according to family size and the level of local wages. The Speenhamland System came to be used all over England, but was much criticised as it resulted in employers keeping wages at a low level, knowing that the difference would be made up by people being forced to undergo the humiliation of applying for assistance from the parish.

THE CLOCK TOWER
c1965 N61090z

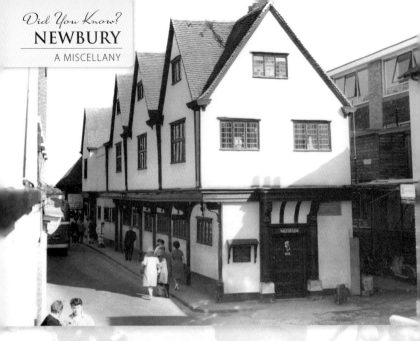

THE MUSEUM c1965 N61302

One of the town's most beautiful buildings, the Cloth Hall, was originally built in the 17th century to provide unemployed weavers with work (see photograph N61302, above). It was restored in 1902 in memory of Queen Victoria and was handed to the Corporation, and later opened as the town museum. It contains exhibitions of local archaeology and natural history, as well as items from the Civil War period and objects relating to the cloth industry and 'Jack O'Newbury', and forms part of the West Berkshire Museum, together with the Granary on the Wharf.

Victoria Park, which lies to the east of Newbury town centre, includes a statue of Queen Victoria guarded by two terracotta lions which originally stood in the Market Place.

The Kennet & Avon Canal, built by the great railway engineer John Rennie, opened in 1810. It linked the Thames to the Bristol Channel via the existing Kennet and Avon river navigations. Like many other canals, its business suffered in competition against the railways, and by the 1950s the canal was sliding into dereliction. Canal enthusiasts successfully fought against its closure and mobilised a voluntary effort to help British Waterways restore it - in 1990 the whole 57 miles (91.7km) again became navigable, and was formally reopened by Her Majesty Queen Elizabeth II. The canal is now used for boating, and walking and cycling are enjoyed along its towpath. At Newbury, grooves can still be seen in the stonework of the canal, cut by the haulage ropes of old horse-drawn craft.

THE RIVER KENNET AND THE CANAL FROM THE BRIDGE c1960 N61103x

The delightful stretch of towpath shown in this photograph, with its lines of quaint cottages and period houses, is where the Kennet & Avon Canal enters Newbury on its way to meet the Thames at Reading. The brick and timber-framed weavers'

cottages are Jacobean, and the tile-hung east gable, partly visible on the extreme left, has moulded bargeboards and a picturesque oriel window which retains its old casements and leaded lights.

THE WEAVERS' COTTAGES AND THE CANAL c1955 N61028

Did You Know?
NEWBURY
A MISCELLANY

THE WHARF c1960 N61105

MARKET PLACE 1952 N61024

At the height of the canal era, the Wharf was a bustling depot where up to ten large barges could load and unload. The long, galleried granary, shown in photograph N61105, opposite, possibly dates back to the reign of Charles II, and is now part of the West Berkshire Museum.

One of the famous names in Newbury's industrial story is that of William Plenty, who founded an engineering firm in 1790 which originally made ploughs. He developed a design for a new, improved lifeboat called the Plenty, which was produced by the firm. After the formation of the National Institution for the Preservation of Life from Shipwreck (later the RNLI) in 1824, Plenty lifeboats were ordered for many of the early lifeboat stations. There are no existing plans or models of the earliest Plenty lifeboats, but a contemporary painting survives of one which was built for Skegness. The essential features of the Plenty lifeboats were the large internal aircases, thick cork sheathing on the outside lower hull and a missing strake just under the rails which facilitated the rolling out of water. The Plenty firm is still in business in Newbury, and now produces pumps and filters.

The old Beynon's store can be seen in the view of the Market Place shown in photograph N61024, opposite. The shop was established in 1827; at one time, lady customers at the store were welcomed with a glass of wine, while the men were offered a glass of ale.

The Second World War affected Newbury in no small way. Air raid sirens were sounded on 244 occasions, and in February 1943 a hit-and-run raid cost lives and property (see page 32). Even the Kennet & Avon Canal played a key role in the war. Along the banks of the waterway, indestructible concrete shelters were positioned - the canal was to act as part of Britain's second line of defence if the enemy invaded the country and breached the south coast blockade. Elliott's of Newbury made thousands of glider planes for wartime use, and Greenham Common (see below) became an airbase for the US 101st Airborne Division, which left from the base on glider sorties during the Normandy landings in 1944.

On the high ground above the valley, just outside Newbury, an area of open common land was acquired by the Air Ministry in 1941 for use as a military base, home first to British squadrons and then the United States Air Force. In 1951 the Americans set about building the longest military runway in Europe at Greenham. In the early 1980s the nuclear-armed Cruise missiles arrived, making Greenham Common a focus of world attention. With CND rallies and peace women camped at the main gates, for a time the controversial airbase was rarely out of the news. The place came to symbolise the uncertainty of the Cold War period and the threat of nuclear attack. Eventually the Cruise missiles went, the derelict buildings were demolished and the perimeter fence taken down. Thanks to a £7 million package, Greenham Common is now being restored to its pre-Second World War state.

ST JOHN'S CHURCH c1965 N61088

On 10 February 1943, enemy action in the shape of a hit-and-run raid by a single Dornier plane caused a great deal of damage in Newbury. Fifteen people died, including elderly women and young children. Nearly 300 shops, houses and various other buildings were damaged, some so badly that they had to be demolished, among them St John's Church. Photograph N61088, above, shows the new church that was built to replace it.

Thatcham, just outside Newbury, has grown and expanded enormously in recent years, although the character of the village remains intact. A flourishing market was once held here, though in the 12th century it was sabotaged by Newbury traders, who were jealous of its success and overturned the market stalls.

The parish church of St Mary at Thatcham dates from about 1141, though much restoration work was carried out during the Victorian era (see photograph T222011, below). Between 1969 and 1970 the tower of this church was renovated, involving the removal of the pinnacles. Two new bells were hung and dedicated to former bell-ringers.

THATCHAM, THE CHURCH c1955 T222011

Inside St Mary's Church at Thatcham is the tomb of a well-known local man, Francis Baily. Baily was a founder member of the Astronomical Society and later became its president. He discovered 'Baily's beads' - gaseous particles in the sun's corona. He also carried out experiments to determine the weight and

THATCHAM, THE WAR MEMORIAL c1955 T222006

density of the earth. Baily's family turned down an offer to have him buried in Westminster Abbey when he died in 1844. Instead they chose a simple tomb in a Berkshire village. He is commemorated in the name of the Francis Baily Primary School in Thatcham.

NORTHBROOK STREET c1955 N61062

BARTHOLOMEW STREET c1965 N61116

Census records show that in 1801 the total population of the West Berkshire area was 34,858; in 1901 it had risen to 50,580, and by 2001 the population was 144,445. By contrast, better healthcare, nutrition and lifestyles has resulted in the rate of infant mortality declining over the same period: the census for 1851 found that 111 babies in every thousand in West Berkshire died in their first year; by 1911 the number had gone down to 76 in every thousand, and by the 2001 census the rate was 7 in every thousand.

One of the famous local tales of Newbury is the story of the Newbury Coat. In 1811 a bet of a thousand guineas was made between Sir John Throckmorton and John Coxeter, a local cloth manufacturer from Greenham, on whether a gentleman's coat could be produced in a single day, from the shearing of the wool from the sheep at 5am to the wearing of the finished coat to dinner at 8pm on the same day. Mr Coxeter claimed that this was possible because of recent developments in machinery in the textile industry. The feat was duly attempted near Greenham Mills, and the local people enjoyed a holiday so that the event might be witnessed. The shorn wool was washed, stubbed, roved, spun and woven; the cloth was then scoured, fulled, tented (stretched), cropped, dyed (a dark damson colour) and dressed by 4pm, and then passed to the tailor, James White, who had already taken Sir John's measurements. Mr White and nine other men then spent the next two hours cutting, stitching and pressing the coat, sewing on buttons and converting the cloth into a 'well woven, properly made coat', which was presented to Sir John at 6.20pm. Sir John put on the coat before a crowd of 5,000 people and sat down to dinner with 40 gentlemen promptly at 8pm. The wager had been won with nearly two hours to spare. The coat is now kept in the Throckmorton family home at Coughton Court in Warwickshire. In 1991 the feat was attempted again at the Newbury Show, and the garment was produced in the same way but beat the time by one hour; this replica coat is now on display in the West Berkshire Museum in Newbury.

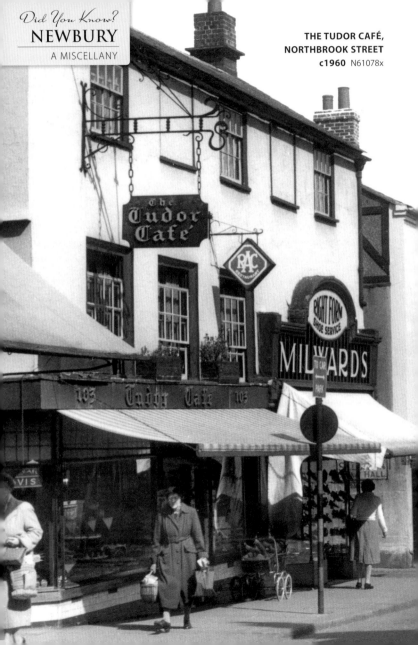

THE TUDOR CAFÉ,
NORTHBROOK STREET
c1960 N61078x

SPORTING NEWBURY

Newbury Rugby Club was founded as far back as 1928. However, the club's greatest successes have come in recent times. One spectacular season was 1996/97, when the first team won National Division 4 South with a 100% win record.

Richard Borgnis, who was born in the town in 1910, had a short but impressive cricket career. A naval officer, he played just one first-class match, for the Combined Services against the New Zealand tourists in 1937. Borgnis scored 101 in the first innings, and followed that by being joint top scorer in the second innings. When New Zealand batted for the first time, he took three wickets. After his one remarkable match, his chances of further top class cricket were halted by the Second World War, and poor health.

AFC Newbury has had a short but eventful history. The club was founded in 1996 when three existing clubs merged. In its first season the club won the Hampshire League, and quickly became a force in the Wessex League, finishing 3rd on two occasions.

Probably the finest athlete to appear for Newbury Athletics Club is Jon Solly. Solly was a superb long distance runner, and the pinnacle of his career was the Edinburgh Commonwealth Games of 1986, where he won the 10,000 metres gold medal.

Many top races, both flat and National Hunt, are run at Newbury racecourse, which celebrated its 100th anniversary in 2005; one of the most popular is always the Hennessy Cognac Gold Cup, a steeplechase run in the autumn. Many top-class steeplechasers have run in the event, but undoubtedly the most famous was the legendary Arkle. An Irish horse, Arkle is widely considered to have been the greatest of all steeplechasers. He won the race on two occasions, in 1964 and 1965. Newbury was also the venue of one of his rare failures, defeat in the 1963 race to Mill House, which was probably due to Arkle slipping on landing after jumping a fence.

QUIZ QUESTIONS

Answers on page 49.

1. What was the name of the Celtic tribe that occupied the Newbury area at the time of the Roman Conquest in the first century AD?

2. The River Kennet and the Kennet & Avon Canal flow through the centre of the town, but two other rivers are associated with Newbury - which are they?

3. Newbury is twinned with which four places?

4. The most important race in the calendar at Newbury racecourse is the Hennessey Cognac Gold Cup. In which month is it run?

5. What does the name 'Newbury' mean?

6. The creator of which much-loved bear was born in Newbury in 1926?

7. Newbury features in which of Thomas Hardy's novels?

8. By what name is the old Globe Inn better known nowadays?

9. What are 'Jack Cloughs', and where in Newbury were they used?

10. Which fictional work about the adventures of a group of rabbits was set on the downs south of Newbury, near the village of Kingsclere?

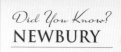

RECIPE

BERKSHIRE HOG

Ingredients

4 pork chops, wiped and
trimmed
300ml/½ pint white wine or
good stock
150ml/5fl oz pint single cream
110g/4oz mushrooms, wiped
and sliced

1 tablespoonful oil
25g/1oz butter
8 shallots or very small onions,
peeled
1bouquet garni
1 tablespoonful plain flour
Salt and freshly ground black
pepper

Heat the butter and oil in a frying pan. Add the pork chops and
lightly brown them on each side. Remove the pork chops, add the
sliced onions to the pan and gently cook until golden. Add the wine
or stock and the bouquet garni. Return the pork chops to the frying
pan, bring the liquid to the boil, cover and simmer gently for 45-60
minutes. Add the sliced mushrooms and cook for 10 minutes.

Mix the flour with a little of the cream. Remove the pan from the
heat and carefully stir in the flour and cream mixture. Return the pan
to the heat, bring to the boil and boil for one minute, stirring all the
time. Add the remainder of the cream, stirring well to heat through,
but do not allow to boil. Remove the bouquet garni, adjust the
seasoning and serve.

NORTHBROOK STREET c1965 N61115

THE TOWN BRIDGE 1956 N61081

YE SWAN INN c1955 N61052

RECIPE

BROAD BEAN AND BACON SOUP

This recipe is reminiscent of the custom of electing the Mayor of Bartlemas (the feast of St Bartholomew) which was still observed in Newbury in the early 19th century on Mace Monday (the first Monday after 25 or 26 July). After the election at a town inn, a dinner of bacon and beans was served. (See David Nash Ford's 'Royal Berkshire History', www.berkshirehistory.com)

Ingredients

225g/8oz shelled broad beans
225g/8oz shelled peas
1 large onion, chopped
450ml/¾ pint milk
300ml/½ pint vegetable stock
2 rashers back bacon, rinded, grilled and chopped

Simmer the beans, peas, onions, milk and stock together for 20 minutes, until the vegetables are tender. Serve the soup garnished with bacon.

The soup can be wholly or partly liquidised if preferred, after which it should be reheated gently, with the bacon garnish added before serving.

QUIZ ANSWERS

1. The Newbury area was in the territory of the Atrebates tribe. Their tribal capital was called Calleva Atrebatum by the Romans, which became the Roman town of Silchester, near Reading.

2. The River Lambourn forms part of Newbury's northern boundary and its southern boundary is formed by the River Enborne.

3. Newbury is twinned with Braunfels in Germany, Bagnols-sur-Cèze in France, Eeklo in Belgium and Feltre in Italy.

4. The Hennessey Cognac Gold Cup is run in November.

5. The name of Newbury means 'New Borough', and the town was probably founded by the lord of the manor, Arnulf de Hesdin, in the 1070s, after the Norman Conquest, in an attempt to develop commerce and trade in the area. Previously there was an Anglo-Saxon village in the area which was known as Ulverton (or Ulvritone).

6. Michael Bond, the creator of Paddington Bear.

7. Newbury features in Thomas Hardy's 'Jude the Obscure', disguised as 'Kennetbridge'. In the novel, Jude came to the town to visit the composer of a hymn.

8. The Globe Inn is now called the Snooty Fox, in Bartholomew Street.

9. 'Jack Cloughs' are lever-operated ground paddles which were used at Newbury Lock, the first lock to be built (in 1796) on the Kennet & Avon Canal. Newbury Lock, near the Lock, Stock & Barrel pub, was the only lock on the canal to use 'Jack Cloughs'.

10. 'Watership Down', by Richard Adams, first published in 1972.

FRANCIS FRITH

PIONEER VICTORIAN PHOTOGRAPHER

Francis Frith, founder of the world-famous photographic archive, was a complex and multi-talented man. A devout Quaker and a highly successful Victorian businessman, he was philosophical by nature and pioneering in outlook. By 1855 he had already established a wholesale grocery business in Liverpool, and sold it for the astonishing sum of £200,000, which is the equivalent today of over £15,000,000. Now in his thirties, and captivated by the new science of photography, Frith set out on a series of pioneering journeys up the Nile and to the Near East.

INTRIGUE AND EXPLORATION

He was the first photographer to venture beyond the sixth cataract of the Nile. Africa was still the mysterious 'Dark Continent', and Stanley and Livingstone's historic meeting was a decade into the future. The conditions for picture taking confound belief. He laboured for hours in his wicker dark-room in the sweltering heat of the desert, while the volatile chemicals fizzed dangerously in their trays. Back in London he exhibited his photographs and was 'rapturously cheered' by members of the Royal Society. His reputation as a photographer was made overnight.

VENTURE OF A LIFE-TIME

By the 1870s the railways had threaded their way across the country, and Bank Holidays and half-day Saturdays had been made obligatory by Act of Parliament. All of a sudden the working man and his family were able to enjoy days out, take holidays, and see a little more of the world.

With typical business acumen, Francis Frith foresaw that these new tourists would enjoy having souvenirs to commemorate their days out. For the next thirty years he travelled the country by train and by pony and trap, producing fine photographs of seaside resorts and beauty spots that were keenly bought by millions of Victorians. These prints were painstakingly pasted into family albums and pored over during the dark nights of winter, rekindling precious memories of summer excursions. Frith's studio was soon supplying retail shops all over the country, and by 1890 F Frith & Co had become the greatest specialist photographic publishing company in the world, with over 2,000 sales outlets, and pioneered the picture postcard.

FRANCIS FRITH'S LEGACY

Francis Frith had died in 1898 at his villa in Cannes, his great project still growing. By 1970 the archive he created contained over a third of a million pictures showing 7,000 British towns and villages.

Frith's legacy to us today is of immense significance and value, for the magnificent archive of evocative photographs he created provides a unique record of change in the cities, towns and villages throughout Britain over a century and more. Frith and his fellow studio photographers revisited locations many times down the years to update their views, compiling for us an enthralling and colourful pageant of British life and character.

We are fortunate that Frith was dedicated to recording the minutiae of everyday life. For it is this sheer wealth of visual data, the painstaking chronicle of changes in dress, transport, street layouts, buildings, housing and landscape that captivates us so much today, offering us a powerful link with the past and with the lives of our ancestors.

Computers have now made it possible for Frith's many thousands of images to be accessed almost instantly. The archive offers every one of us an opportunity to examine the places where we and our families have lived and worked down the years. Its images, depicting our shared past, are now bringing pleasure and enlightenment to millions around the world a century and more after his death.

For further information visit: **www.francisfrith.com**

INTERIOR DECORATION

Frith's photographs can be seen framed and as giant wall murals in thousands of pubs, restaurants, hotels, banks, retail stores and other public buildings throughout Britain. These provide interesting and attractive décor, generating strong local interest and acting as a powerful reminder of gentler days in our increasingly busy and frenetic world.

FRITH PRODUCTS

All Frith photographs are available as prints and posters in a variety of different sizes and styles. In the UK we also offer a range of other gift and stationery products illustrated with Frith photographs, although many of these are not available for delivery outside the UK – see our web site for more information on the products available for delivery in your country.

THE INTERNET

Over 100,000 photographs of Britain can be viewed and purchased on the Frith web site. The web site also includes memories and reminiscences contributed by our customers, who have personal knowledge of localities and of the people and properties depicted in Frith photographs. If you wish to learn more about a specific town or village you may find these reminiscences fascinating to browse. Why not add your own comments if you think they would be of interest to others? See **www.francisfrith.com**

PLEASE HELP US BRING FRITH'S PHOTOGRAPHS TO LIFE

Our authors do their best to recount the history of the places they write about. They give insights into how particular towns and villages developed, they describe the architecture of streets and buildings, and they discuss the lives of famous people who lived there. But however knowledgeable our authors are, the story they tell is necessarily incomplete.

Frith's photographs are so much more than plain historical documents. They are living proofs of the flow of human life down the generations. They show real people at real moments in history; and each of those people is the son or daughter of someone, the brother or sister, aunt or uncle, grandfather or grandmother of someone else. All of them lived, worked and played in the streets depicted in Frith's photographs.

We would be grateful if you would give us your insights into the places shown in our photographs: the streets and buildings, the shops, businesses and industries. Post your memories of life in those streets on the Frith website: what it was like growing up there, who ran the local shop and what shopping was like years ago; if your workplace is shown tell us about your working day and what the building is used for now. Read other visitors' memories and reconnect with your shared local history and heritage. With your help more and more Frith photographs can be brought to life, and vital memories preserved for posterity, and for the benefit of historians in the future.

Wherever possible, we will try to include some of your comments in future editions of our books. Moreover, if you spot errors in dates, titles or other facts, please let us know, because our archive records are not always completely accurate—they rely on 140 years of human endeavour and hand-compiled records. You can email us using the contact form on the website.

Thank you!

For further information, trade, or author enquiries please contact us at the address below:

The Francis Frith Collection, Unit 6, Oakley Business Park, Wylye Road, Dinton, Wiltshire SP3 5EU England.
Tel: +44 (0)1722 716 376 Fax: +44 (0)1722 716 881
e-mail: sales@francisfrith.co.uk **www.francisfrith.com**